LIVES AND TIMES

Alexander Graham Bell

Jane Shuter

Heinemann
LIBRARY

www.heinemann.co.uk.

Visit our website to find out more information about **Heinemann Library** books

To order:

☎ Phone ++44 (0)1865 888066

▤ Send a fax to ++44 (0)1865 314091

▢ Visit the Heinemann Bookshop at www.heinemann.co.uk to browse our catalogue and order online.

First published in Great Britain by Heinemann Library,
Halley Court, Jordan Hill, Oxford OX2 8EJ,
a division of Reed Educational and Professional Publishing Ltd.
Heinemann is a registered trademark of Reed Educational & Professional Publishing Limited.

OXFORD MELBOURNE AUCKLAND JOHANNESBURG BLANTYRE
GABORONE IBADAN PORTSMOUTH NH (USA) CHICAGO

Designed by Visual Image
Illustrations by Pamela Goodchild
Originated by Dot Gradations
Printed and bound in Hong Kong/China
04 03 02 01 00
10 9 8 7 6 5 4 3 2 1
ISBN 0 431 023247

British Library Cataloguing in Publication Data

Shuter, Jane
Alexander Graham Bell. – (Lives and Times)
1. Bell, Alexander Graham, 1847–1922 – Juvenile literature 2. Inventor
Britain – Biography – Juvenile literature 3. Telephone – History – Juver
I. Title
621.3'85'092
ISBN 0431023247

Acknowledgements

The Publishers would like to thank the following for permission to reproduce photographs: Alexander Graham Bell Historic Site: pp16, 18, 19, 21, 22; Bridgeman Art Library: p17; Dale Wilson: p23; National Galleries of Scotland: p20.

Cover photograph reproduced with permission of Science Photo Library.

Every effort has been made to contact copyright holders of any material reproduced in this book. Any omissions will be rectified in subsequent printings if notice is given to the Publisher.

Any words appearing in the text in bold, **like this**, are explained in the Glossary.

Contents

Early life

Alexander Graham Bell was born in Scotland on 3 March 1847. Bell's mother was **deaf**. His father helped deaf people to speak clearly.

Bell worked as a teacher. In 1867 he
moved to London to join his father. He
helped work out a new way of teaching
deaf people to speak.

A new life

Bell's brothers both died of **TB**. Bell began to worry about his own health. The family decided to **emigrate** to Canada.
The Bells settled in Brantford, Canada.

Bell and his father then went to work in Boston, USA. In 1872 Bell set up a school in Boston for teachers of the **deaf**.

The telephone

Bell started to think about how to send sounds from place to place along a wire. He and his assistant, Thomas Watson, began work on a telephone in 1873.

On 4 March 1876 Bell **patented** the telephone. Three days later he sent his first spoken message to Watson in another room. In October they had their first two-way talk.

Work with the deaf

Bell was still teaching **deaf** people. In 1877 he married Mabel Hubbard. Mabel had been one of his pupils. In 1880 he won the Volta Prize for his work with the deaf.

Bell used his prize of $10,000 to set up the Volta **Laboratory**. Here his workers improved the **phonograph**, an early record player. This was a big success.

Nova Scotia

In 1886 Bell bought land in Nova Scotia, Canada. He built a house and **laboratories** there. He tried out many new ideas, including flying machines and **solar power**.

In 1898 Bell became president of the
National Geographic Society. He changed
the *National Geographic* magazine, and made
it the first to include a lot of photographs.

Later life

Bell and his wife worked together on flying machines. In 1909 they flew the Silver Dart for the first time. This was their most successful flying machine.

Bell's other successful travel machine was the **hydrofoil**. In 1919 a Bell hydrofoil reached a speed of 70 miles per hour. Bell continued working on inventions all his life. He died on 3 August 1922.

Pictures

There are many ways we can find out about Alexander Graham Bell and his inventions. Photos show us what he and his family and friends looked like.

Paintings show us what Boston looked like when Bell lived there. This painting shows the part of Boston where rich people lived.

Written clues

This is Bell's **patent** for the telephone.

There were arguments in court about it.

The court said the patent belonged to Bell.

Bell's notebook entry for March 10, 1876

Bell's notebooks are full of sketches of inventions. They include telephone **designs** and simple **experiments**. These pages are part of his telephone experiment.

Inventions

This is a **replica** of Alexander Bell's first telephone. At this stage, there were no separate listening and speaking parts. Another inventor, Thomas Edison, **designed** separate parts in 1878.

FULL SIZE REPRODUCTION OF THE
ORIGINAL TELEPHONE INVENTED IN 1875 BY
ALEXANDER GRAHAM BELL
MADE IN POST OFFICE ENGINEERING DEPARTMENTS WORKSHOP
EDINBURGH NOVEMBER 1937.

This is a replica of Bell's **hydrofoil**. It is in
the museum of the Alexander Graham Bell
Historic Site in Baddeck, Canada.

Museums

The Bell house in Brantford, Canada, is now a museum. It has been kept the way it was in Bell's time. Most of the things there belonged to the Bells.

The Alexander Graham Bell Historic Site in Baddeck, Canada, is the museum with the most information about Bell. It has papers, photographs and **replicas** of many of his inventions.

Glossary

This glossary explains difficult words and helps you to say words which may be hard to say.

deaf person who cannot hear, or can only hear a little

design drawings of what something will look like and how it will work

emigrate to leave one country to go to live in another one

experiment trying out ideas to see what happens

hydrofoil boat with underwater wings. You say *hi-dro-foyl*.

laboratory place where people do experiments

patent when a person has a good idea they can go to the patent office, where the idea is given a date and a special number. No one else can use the idea to make money. You say *pay-tent*.

phonograph machine for playing back sounds recorded in grooves on a flat disc. You say *fone-o-graf*.

replica copy of something that looks exactly like it. You say *rep-lick-a*.

solar power using the heat from the Sun to make energy to power machines

TB short for tuberculosis, a disease which affects the lungs

Index

Titles in the *Lives and Times* series include:

Hardback   0 431 02324 7

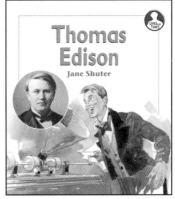

Hardback   0 431 02323 9

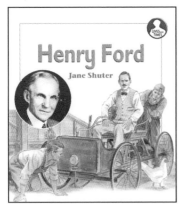

Hardback   0 431 02325 5

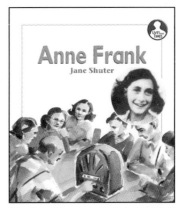

Hardback   0 431 02322 0

Hardback   0 431 02515 0

Find out about the other titles in this series on our website www.heinemann.co.uk/library